Dedicated to:

All who wish to open their heart
and mind, to learn, to grow,
to consider things differently

Joyful Navigations Presents:

Positive Quotes

with

Author Holly

Volume 1

Holly Ruttenbur Dickinson

Positive Quotes with Author Holly, Volume 1
by Holly Ruttenbur Dickinson.

Book of Quotes.

Copyright ©2020 Holly Ruttenbur Dickinson
Joyful Navigations/Trade Name
Joyful Navigations™
Published by Shifting Open LLC.

Self-Help, Personal Growth, Happiness, Success,
Motivational, Inspirational, Soul, Joy

Book Design, Graphics, Quote Design by Holly
Dickinson

Printed in the United States of America

ISBN: 978-1-7355347-1-8

Contents & Content Key Word Topics:

UPLIFT
with words and
actions.
©Holly Ruttenbur Dickinson

When we go
through painful experiences,
it helps us, in turn, to be able
to relate to others when they go
through painful experiences. It helps
us connect on a deeper level.
This is true empathy.
©Holly Ruttenbur Dickinson

Sometimes,
we need to bring
a different kind of clarity
to our perspective.

©Holly Ruttenbur Dickinson

AUTHOR
HOLLY

joyfulnavigations.com

My Smile
runs deeper now.
It doesn't just cover my
face. It emanates from
the Joyfulness in
my Soul.

©Holly Ruttenbur Dickinson

AUTHOR
HOLLY

joyfulnavigations.com

I forgive you.
Saying these words and
feeling them at your core,
is life changing.
©Holly Ruttenbur Dickinson

AUTHOR
HOLLY

joyfulnavigations.com

JOYFUL
is a way of Being.
Not just something
you feel.
©Holly Ruttenbur Dickinson

AUTHOR
HOLLY

joyfulnavigations.com

Simple appreciation goes a long way.

©Holly Ruttenbur Dickinson

joyfulnavigations.com

Sometimes we just need to stop, take a deep breath, and look at the beauty in front of us.

©Holly Ruttenbur Dickinson

joyfulnavigations.com

Thank you for teaching me skills. I was able to turn around and teach others those skills. I am enjoying watching them grow as you watched me grow.

©Holly Ruttenbur Dickinson

Emotional growth helps you SEE a bigger picture, take on a broader mindset, and see different perspectives.

©Holly Ruttenbur Dickinson

Ahhhh...
Could it Be?
All the Jewels
I've searched
My Whole Life for
Have ALWAYS been
Here...
Inside Me?!!

Poem: My Jewels, 2014
©Holly Ruttenbur Dickinson

AUTHOR
HOLLY
joyfulnavigations.com

We are given
our dreams and visions
for reasons we do not yet
comprehend .

©Holly Ruttenbur Dickinson

AUTHOR
HOLLY

joyfulnavigations.com

You can tell your story
from a victim standpoint or you
can share your story from an empowered
growth standpoint... no matter how
traumatic the experience was. How
you tell your story signals where you
are in your growth process.

©Holly Ruttenbur Dickinson

AUTHOR
HOLLY

joyfulnavigations.com

*Destination happiness,
is a misconception. If you
aren't happy NOW, you won't
be happy when you get
THERE, either.*

©Holly Ruttenbur Dickinson

AUTHOR
HOLLY

joyfulnavigations.com

*I'm choosing the state of JOY.
How about you? I've learned
enough from pain and suffering.
They've served their purpose and I've
grown. Now it's time for a shift and
learn, in the state of JOY!*

©Holly Ruttenbur Dickinson

*I ADMIRE and RESPECT
those who are WILLING and
take the inner journey to DO
the WORK necessary to HEAL
their deepest wounds.*

©Holly Ruttenbur Dickinson

> *Sometimes people's beliefs blind them from opening their heart.*
>
> ©Holly Ruttenbur Dickinson
>
> *joyfulnavigations.com*

> *REMEMBER the lessons. They help you to be WISE.*
>
> ©Holly Ruttenbur Dickinson
>
> *joyfulnavigations.com*

For a better world...
It starts with how we
treat ourselves.

©Holly Ruttenbur Dickinson

AUTHOR
HOLLY

Affirmation:
Self-care is VITAL,
in order for ME to RISE
into my GREATEST
potential.

©Holly Ruttenbur Dickinson

AUTHOR
HOLLY

When someone believes in you, REALLY, REALLY believes in you... you feel as if YOU can SOAR!

©Holly Ruttenbur Dickinson

AUTHOR HOLLY

joyfulnavigations.com

The noblest way to live one's life is through kindness and compassion.

©Holly Ruttenbur Dickinson

AUTHOR HOLLY

joyfulnavigations.com

When you apologize...
do it with sincerity of the
heart. Then adjust your
behavior showing that
you truly meant it. That's
a sincere apology.
©Holly Ruttenbur Dickinson

You get through
sadness, pain, or
grieving, one step at a
time. Feel it. And start
filling your life with what
feeds your soul.

And gentleness... don't
forget to be gentle on you.
©Holly Ruttenbur Dickinson

*It's not magic...
it's hard work on oneself.
That's what makes
the difference.*

©Holly Ruttenbur Dickinson

AUTHOR
HOLLY

joyfulnavigations.com

*Emotional healing
brings emotional
freedom and
emotional growth.*

©Holly Ruttenbur Dickinson

AUTHOR
HOLLY

joyfulnavigations.com

*We attract
what energy/vibe
we put out.*

©Holly Ruttenbur Dickinson

*Kindness
expands our
heart space.*

©Holly Ruttenbur Dickinson

*Every ACT
has energy to it.
Best if we make it
KIND and positive
energy.*

©Holly Ruttenbur Dickinson

AUTHOR
HOLLY

*Only YOU,
can change
YOU!*

©Holly Ruttenbur Dickinson

AUTHOR
HOLLY

Our attitude about each experience determines how much growth we gain from each experience.

©Holly Ruttenbur Dickinson

AUTHOR
HOLLY

joyfulnavigations.com

With HOPE and ACTION, you will get there.

©Holly Ruttenbur Dickinson

AUTHOR
HOLLY

joyfulnavigations.com

Perspectives consistently need adjustment because we are consistently changing with every life experience.

©Holly Ruttenbur Dickinson

joyfulnavigations.com

The ordinary, mundane, and routine, have shown me some of my greatest JOYS. I realized it was all in the way I was seeing it. Perspective, really is Everything!!

©Holly Ruttenbur Dickinson

joyfulnavigations.com

This life is but a short time. We learn what our souls came here to learn. We do what our souls came here to do.

©Holly Ruttenbur Dickinson

AUTHOR HOLLY

joyfulnavigations.com

What I perceive as JOYFUL, may be different than what it may be for you. What is JOYFUL to one, is as diverse as the individuals we are.

©Holly Ruttenbur Dickinson

AUTHOR HOLLY

joyfulnavigations.com

God celebrates us, sees our
personal potential, and wants us to
celebrate ourselves too. How can we
love our neighbor as ourselves if we
aren't loving and celebrating ourselves?
Celebrate You!! God Does!!

©Holly Ruttenbur Dickinson

AUTHOR
HOLLY

joyfulnavigations.com

*Work on yourself,
to become your BEST self.
And... be KIND and
LOVING to yourself.*

©Holly Ruttenbur Dickinson

AUTHOR
HOLLY

joyfulnavigations.com

I forgive you.
I forgive me.
Let's move
forward.

©Holly Ruttenbur Dickinson

joyfulnavigations.com

Pointing a finger
is more about ourselves,
I've learned. Do our own
inner work FIRST.

©Holly Ruttenbur Dickinson

joyfulnavigations.com

You ARE a beautiful soul and I'm here to remind YOU of that.

©Holly Ruttenbur Dickinson

joyfulnavigations.com

I inspire, because it LIFTS SOULS.

©Holly Ruttenbur Dickinson

joyfulnavigations.com

> *Those daily small steps, sometimes take the BIGGEST COURAGE.*
>
> *©Holly Ruttenbur Dickinson*

joyfulnavigations.com

> *I had to take ACTION, serious action, for my inner world to change. As painful as the process was, it's the GREATEST thing I've ever done for MYSELF!!*
>
> *©Holly Ruttenbur Dickinson*

joyfulnavigations.com

Thank you for the No's.
Thank you for the "real talk", your cruelty.
Thank you for the emotional pain.
Thank you for the sadness.
Thank you for the rejection.
Thank you for the abandonment.
These behaviors taught me to turn to myself and:
To start saying Yes to myself.
To treat myself kindly.
To go on a journey to heal my pain.
To create my own Happiness and JOY.
To fully accept, love, and cherish myself.
To be my greatest cheerleader, my own best friend,
and to not abandon myself... Ever!
Your example taught me the greatest lessons.

©Holly Ruttenbur Dickinson

Choose to GROW.

©Holly Ruttenbur Dickinson

AUTHOR
HOLLY

*Some people expect
God, to do it all for them.
But, God, expects us to move
our feet and take action.
Then, He helps.*

©Holly Ruttenbur Dickinson

AUTHOR
HOLLY

joyfulnavigations.com

*When my INNER world
is calm, the chaos outside
seems less extreme.*

©Holly Ruttenbur Dickinson

AUTHOR
HOLLY

joyfulnavigations.com

*A walk in any
NATURE,
no matter how
vast or how small, is
healing, renewing,
and refreshing.*

©Holly Ruttenbur Dickinson

AUTHOR
HOLLY

*Staying in the
present, in the moment,
is to truly experience
something in the
richest way.*

©Holly Ruttenbur Dickinson

AUTHOR
HOLLY

Empathy and compassion are the keys to true connection.

©Holly Ruttenbur Dickinson

When people say you're too sensitive, much of the time it's an excuse used for not having good communication between the two people and an excuse to not speak kindness.

©Holly Ruttenbur Dickinson

I used to always look for the big, the remarkable, to find my happiness. It was never enough. When I healed inside me, my wounds, the simple and routine became the greatest beauty and it was enough. Healing, brought awakening to the greatest beauty, and JOY in the most simple.

©Holly Ruttenbur Dickinson

Be watchful of YOUR focus.

©Holly Ruttenbur Dickinson

Change =

Awareness +
Decision +
Action.

©*Holly Ruttenbur Dickinson*

To change YOUR life,
your habits, or your direction...
It takes Awareness, then a
Decision, then Action!

©*Holly Ruttenbur Dickinson*

*Pay attention
to the
promptings.*

©Holly Ruttenbur Dickinson

AUTHOR
HOLLY

*Sometimes, you
have to put things,
people, at a distance
so you can find
YOURSELF.*

©Holly Ruttenbur Dickinson

AUTHOR
HOLLY

When we can treat
one another as equals; not
better or less than, but "of value",
then we can achieve our greatest
as a society. A treasured society
or community would be where
everyone feels valued.

©Holly Ruttenbur Dickinson

We are stronger and
wiser and far more influential
when we use that "influence"
with great KINDNESS. Cruelty
has no place in hearts.

©Holly Ruttenbur Dickinson

A Message from the Author

Thank you for reading my first little book of quotes. It is my intention to bring forth several additional volumes. Volume 2 has already been started. I hope that something in my writings has inspired you and/or brought some new awareness to your thinking. Maybe it has given you some new perspectives to consider, prompted growth or prompted changed behavior. Hopefully something here has helped you smile, brought you joy, or set you on a journey to become a better you.

~Author Holly, Your Joyful Guide

Visit me on the Facebook Page: *Positive Quotes with Author Holly* and *Choose Joyful with Joyful Navigations™ or joyfulnavigations.com*

About the Author

Author Holly R. Dickinson is a Light Worker and a Mass Influencer of 7 million plus followers on her Facebook Page. She is a Mother of 4, now adults. She is in a loving marriage to her husband of 27 years. Early life brought many traumas and challenges to her. She shares her wisdom, perspectives, and courage in her writings. God, love, kindness, awareness, courage, action, compassion, forgiveness, self-care, positivity, and choosing joy are key for her.